Threshold State

Threshold State

Poems by

Phyllis Stowell

© 2022 Phyllis Stowell. All rights reserved.
This material may not be reproduced in any form, published,
reprinted, recorded, performed, broadcast,
rewritten or redistributed without
the explicit permission of Phyllis Stowell.
All such actions are strictly prohibited by law.

Cover design by Shay Culligan

Cover Image by Pacia Sallomi, Arrangements 2
from the series *Immanence* oil on wood

Author photograph by Deborah O'Grady

ISBN: 978-1-63980-102-2

Kelsay Books
502 South 1040 East, A-119
American Fork, Utah 84003
Kelsaybooks.com

For my grandchildren
Galen, Megan, William
my great-granddaughter Clemence
and you

Acknowledgments

Without the careful reading and insightful observations by the members of our poetry group, which for thirty years has included Alan Williamson, Peter Dale Scott, and Sandra M. Gilbert, and now also includes Jeanne Foster, Beverly Bie Brachic, Katie Peterson, and David Shaddock. Various wonderful guests have brought fresh perspectives, which help to keep us from ossified reactions.

As with all my books, I am grateful for my daughter Pacia Sallomi's permission to use her art for the cover of *Threshold State*. In addition, I value her intelligent reading of some of the poems, which provides a special vitality to my writing life.

Many thanks to Joyce Jenkins for a book-launch Zoom reading with Katie Peterson in the Poetry Flash series. In addition, my gratitude to Steven Fus, President of the Analytical Psychology Club of San Francisco, for the opportunity to present a reading and Q & A of this manuscript.

Finally, I am deeply moved by the fellowship and regard that Colleen Lix, my successor as Director of the Friends of the San Francisco Jungian Institute, has given me, including an opportunity to present: Creative Writing as Soul Work.

Also by Phyllis Stowell

POETRY BOOKS

Ascent to Solitude
Arc of Grief
Engraved Tablet
SHIELD/Bouclier
SUNDERED
A Cast of Coins
Einstein's Knot

CHAPBOOKS

Who is Alice?
Emergence

ANTHOLOGY
Co-editor

APPETITE:
Food as Metaphor
An anthology of Women Poets

NON-FICTION

TRANSFORMATIONS
Nearing the End of Life:
Dreams and Visions

Contents

Radical Absorption

Reckoning	17
Earthly Vision	19
Assignation	20
Intimation	21
Aubade	22
At Eighty-eight	23
Flame	24

Signature

Sleep	29
Orator	30
Hymn	32
Unlike	34
The Turn	35
Between Here and There	37
Signature	39

The Light in the Eye

Old Folks Home	43
Vastation	45
One Night Two Givens	47
Radiance Remembered	48
The Light in the Eye	49
Havoc	55

East Wind

The Present	59
Faith of Our Fathers	60
Family	61
Reverie	62
Virtue	63
Death	64
Relic	66
Love and Dust	67
Kuan Yin	68
Mind Miniatures	70
Beyond Good and Evil	73
To a Friend Who Translated the Bhagavad Gita	75
The Library	76
Not Hopper	77
East Wind	78
Preface	80
Against Entropy	81
Fog	83
Meditation on The Big Bang	84
Aubade II	85

Little Season

What Dwells Within	89
By Birth Conferred	90
Extricate Yourself	91
Psilocybin	93
Spirit	95
My Slipper	96
Clumsy	97

Penitent	98
Gnosis	99
Candor	100
At the Verge	101
Daylight	105
The Expectation	106

*The day draws near, it cannot be far off;
time runs and files so far*
—Petrarch

Radical Absorption

It may be a mere vague enthusiasm, half spiritual, half vital, a courage, and a feeling that great and wondrous things are in the air
—William James

Reckoning

Your mind teams with reincarnations   what happened
happens againandagain   *Past* is never passed

Why then is old age a cage you like a panther pace

Don't you comprehend yet? Each act   once done
can never change   Your longing is ashes

I'll tell you what old age is

When sun breaks through morning fog your sight is blinded
while a one-note coloratura repeats and repeats in your ear

Old means limitations galore
Daily you knock against a new one you never imagined

as when you pick up a box of waste paint   that fire hazard
would spin your spine out of orbit

You never imagined that your cat   a mewing infant still
would grow too heavy to lift or carry

You never imagined that your writing hand
would cramp with the claw-disease

that nightly your legs would wake up
nervy lullaby in a log-jam of ice

Old age   *really old*   others admire you for moving
ask what brands you brought to buy them when you aren't

Old offers time alone
when it's divine to be alone

There's no bitterness at being unknown – oh yes
being known and dismissed   *that* poison cannot kill

Blissfully painting with pungent oils by Mother's hearth
accompanied by Mahler

not even imagining others coincident in your dimension
you were wholly consumed – a radical absorption

Writing these words   do you *really* have others in mind?
Admit it – talking to yourself is a widow's way

or say   *pleasure*

Earthly Vision

Then I eased down into dirt
to soothe my body
a coin of heat at the top of my skull

where the chakra might have been
no soul blast upward
into the Thousand Petals

I lay pulled down
by a mild magnetic force   then
as if from the crown of my head

streamed three amorphous forms
each larger than the one preceding
emitting amber light

Assignation

I'll meet you in forty years at P'eng Mountain
                                        —*Shang-yin*

A poet's allusion—Mt. P'eng-lai
island of Immortals
            and the elixir of life

We'll meet there
Seems forty years

ten mountains and a thousand
bridges crossed

no sooner arrived
ten more mountains rise

In the Shades the dead whisper
Unite the lovers
            almost a summons

coupled so often in dreams

Intimation

His poise could not conceal tremors
nor could the poem he read

in a sick man's gentle graveled voice
as if the vowels had been soothed

by some untold mystery for it seemed
a woman spoke through him

What she revealed I can barely recall
except in a dream that followed

a radiance
seeping through a doorframe

wherein all would be sweet-smelling air
and equipoise

What transpired between us—strangers—
when his look afflicted with the slow

turning downward into death
prevailed in me—a knowledge

that I had no notion of
a passion I could not endure

Aubade

Days you slept till ten
drugged by medications paired with wine

Each wary-waking made explicit
yesterday's docility did not harm or heal

Each breath began nothing   each step went nowhere
with a needy friend your voice could not conceal
its vexed edge

A belated aubade hums what must be done
despite the grimace of an elderly cripple

who twisting her head up sidewise
to squint at your face   said *You were*

—then her silence said
a shred of what you had been

On the left hand where the rings were
sunheat warns

Already it is evening
and either melancholy nor revelry
alters your fate

At Eighty-eight

It has become familiar
You feel it through the mattress—a tremor

and the way it
lurches toward you in a fall

Do you fear the Death Demon
who relishes the taste of living skin

One Nordic tribe's sacred rite
preemptively cut their old ones up

Abiding beneath a cool celadon sun
another had no fear—none!

for at the great bar piled high with eatables
the drunk dead feast

He has Mephistophelian skills
Don't think for a moment He isn't real!

Consider the evidence
Walking you catch yourself talking to the absent

Passing by He smirks
Whenever there's a pause   He interrupts

Flame

The flame lit up
flooding the room

with flickering shadows
wavering light

touching Quan Yin
her carved eyebrows

hint of smile
She was experiencing—what?

Is the contemplative
complicit?

Some inbetween
To drift there unprevented

white   whale white
eponymous phantom

seamind where the givens
are not caught in that slow downward vortex

At *that*
the flame went out

on second thought
—the absolute unnerving—

budded a bit   sputtered
muttering to itself

brightened briefly
then discreetly died

flared up   a startle look
then all went blatant black

Signature

*A piece of wood, uncarved, natural, cannot
be used by anyone. The leaders who can be genuine
and natural as this gain the respect of the people.*
—TAO TE CHING

Sleep

Damne me, it's worth a fellow's while
to be born into the world, if only to fall right asleep.
            —Stubb
            Moby-Dick

A fellow afflicted   beset   pleaded
that these years he cannot   cannot get to sleep

Of an age when women no longer compete to claim him
you judged he'd grown afraid of what within him stirs

As if to punish you for presumption that night
you stared wide awake at the command   SLEEP

a prelude to night after bedeviled night when nothing
specific worries you   while your teaming braincells

wear out streaming irrelevancies
like the futile two-hour argument at the freeway edge

with a highway cop who blamed you
for being old and white   female and by a fool rear-ended

Mind has a basketful of snarled snaky
injustices to drawn on

Body tries another position   sits up   meditates
moves to the sofa   then back to tiresome bed

Your friend found her sister dead   half in bed
half on the floor   one arm extended   reaching

What makes you want to crawl under the rug
headfirst   the way the cat does?

Orator

...he drilled deep down; and blasted all my reason out of me!
...Will I, nill I, the ineffable thing has tied me to him; tows me
  with a cable I have no knife to cut.
                                        —Starbuck

In the beginning he speaks solely to you
for you can only hear
not question

By tone and cadence
by melodrama of the spoken word
even a prudent man might cheer for him
who gives his approval   the seed that gratifies
parent to our child

By stages he persuades
until his face a grimace of manic intent
And what tune is it ye pull to, men?
in unison all come together
in fused hate

He can quell suppress dispel
our effort to manage malice   betrayal
a thousand wrongs
All he needs to say is
this is good   that is bad

It's bad to put me on trial for what I did
It hurts me   I plead with you
my hurt is your hurt

And all good fellows in unison shout
A dead whale or a stove boat!

A demagogue is master of the masses
and the masses   who are they?   even a moral man
assailed by splenetic speech   beset by doubt
can into delusion from confusion
to confusion fall

Hymn

What if the sovereign himself is the villainous destroyer of the realm?
—Li Shang-yin
Scholar of the Jade Stream

Oh America! God send his grace
greatly needed grace

Save us from this specter
this mind-maimed captain of our careening ship

whose lunacy squalls
from sea to darkening sea

his wrath an infant impotency
disguised by braggadocio

who knows full well it's all an act
smug because to all he has dissembled

This is his pride   his talent   his reality

He is deceived
possessed by Powers beyond his powers

like Ahab   underneath Ahab
deep in unconscious seas

an unseen god grips and swirls him
dragging him down

In delusion he tweets he would attack the sun
if the sun offended him

as so many have offended him

Cheering crowds
masked gunmen   renegades

righteous true believers
genuine heroes and jolly simple folk

all benighted

How is it we respond
embracing or appalled

ourselves possessed
until his hate becomes ours

his crew   sycophants
a few afraid of loss cling to gunwales

The best flounder like fish upon the dock
The rest bent on profitable cruises

paid for by the public mint
All discount this sinking Ship

Unlike

As if—near the end of my days—I stepped into a stream mid-stream
unable to move forward toward an impervious destiny nor go back
    where my beloved's death was my sole absolute

Returning in rainy night mist I stalled at the threshold listening to
fizzles of rainwater
tapping fallen amber-tree leaves   content   as if December's
penetrating cold
     existed to prove me wrong

As it lightens I sit and wait like the lean tensed form of the pianist
crabbed over the keys
intensity fiercely held against liminal divide—not yet not yet—his
body jerked back
     again   not yet

The Turn

Missed the turn—how surprising! We turned around
   descending then turning left passing a sign
Don't park in the drive!

We passed the five houses   only the last enlarged
   lot-edge to lot-edge   ahead
the expansive entrance to Lane'sEnd

I'd fantasized meeting the wife at the front door
   explaining I wanted my granddaughter to see
what she   being too young   did not recall

an interior with glorious hand-sanded woods
   spaciousness with stained glass above the door
casting colors on the entry floor   like a chapel

Ahead the white vinyl garage door   filthy and rusted
   a pealing water tank in the side drive   no plants
but one resistant vine I'd embedded behind the retaining wall

All shut   locked up as if unoccupied
   the exterior once natural dove grey   a nauseating baby blue
the northside decks stained shit-brown

Needing to see the rock rose under which I buried
   Jerry's ashes—he so loved the house we'd designed—
I walked between garage and uphill wall

to encounter a waste of wild scrub   our hot tub
   long gone   a few rotting boards   and the scratchy-leafed
untended rock rose beside a wild half-dead shrub

On the corner deck railing perched a wooden owl
   that with the wind turned its head
and unblinking eye

Between Here and There

Between here and there one elongated time
   that began at the farthest reach
lava black pinnacles of rock
   minarets thrust skyward
merging with wind scoured boulders
   blocking passage north northwest
where you headed down the long beach
   you and sea and wet sand
willets a-dither at the foam edge of receding wave
   risking the liminal moment of return
a few picnic tables up-slope by the leveling
   where all come down
from the cluster of unlike cottages and No Parking signs
   past women leashed to dog companions
two bulky-jacketed Latinos   one on his cell phone
   bursting laughter
the older other looking down   bored or sad
   farther on fewer came
stink   a six-foot decay
   seal head turned as if pillowed
eyeless with a look of longing
   its pinkish tail intact   almost alive
a crow furiously tugging at an unyielding
   gut tendon
footprints dwindled to pawprints   then
   just sand and snarled hair
you went beyond your strength   faster
   despite your cane digging in
you went with an urgency you did not
   attempt to comprehend
inlandward the beach widened in ash hued ripples
   like driedout ocean floor

the grass-skulled dune lowered   opposite the waters
    rose a wall of shade-green
a patch of beachgray beneath a lone dome-shaped tree
    waveless shore
here diminishing waves   water greening
   midway the surface strangely stalled
                          above the hidden mingling
the glazed black body of seal arcing   then another
   a duck bobbing in swells and subsides
the low dune lengthened to the dark wet edge
    a narrow ledge   a bank you stepped around
beheld the broad estuary
   cradled in bluff and viridians
the river disappearing in misty blue hills
                                  beyond
wild imaginings
   but for the sign
Lawson's Landing   in red
    at the left bank cove

Signature

Listening...we don't.
The inner conversation never stops.
It's a constant racket
          —Philip Glass

Almost breathless having raced as by hazard late
I sat down in my balcony mid-center seat
just as Pinchas Zukerman   assured yet with halting steps
approached the podium

What did I expect? Nineteenth Century classics
so familiar no need to read Program Notes   How explain
what began with Beethoven's brooding sostenuto
not that timely expression of Egmont's fatal protest against a tyrant
but the sustained perfection contained like a fist in poise
every performer   every instrument   every pause
held by the conductor's restraint and his hands' explosive power
The composer's nerve-jarring passion came full
and all the hall felt one

Then I curved my hands around my face
alone on a high-cliff   an ocelot's eye
watching the brass in a blazing arc tier above tier
each instrument   each motion
even the lean first violinist's wrist
the concerto Mozart's fifth   the performers
listening each to each with impeccable ear
Zukerman magically turning with his violin
becoming the strings   bowing with such verve and precision
it seemed he improvised
then the adagio's resonance of cellos and double-basses
a passage that struck heart's minor chord

struck again when Tchaikovsky's 5th Symphony—his last
but one before his suicide—began
somber bassoons and clarinets sounding steps heavy with time
a prolonged *andante andante andante*
Midway the drummer danced between his drums
then the final drumroll

As if to explain the profundity of consonance
that night reading the last page of *Psyche und Tod*
a woman's dreams during the war   tortured and dark
then she beheld a time-faded gift from one of
Deutschland's esteemed conductors   an etching
> on the bottom left a scene of cruelty
> on the right souls rising up out of the earth
> rising to Death the Fiddler

its signature: *Tchaikovsky's 5th*

The Light in the Eye

*Will it not call for the whole duration of the
centuries before our sight is attuned to the light?*
—Pierre Teilhard de Chardin

Old Folks Home

This is the room watered by moving light
where sound-and-fury is false gold

Drought-resistant I have become
an alphabet that can't be transmuted

Here is the last map of my life
a table with an incense holder   a trance

the hypnotic rhythm of silence
In a dream of temperate air

strangers care for grandmother
shoved into a closet in a wheel chair

she presses her splayed hands
flat against the facing wall

willful and embattled
I've read tons of books

word by silently sounded word
as if slowness would elicit profundity

Nothing memorized
but phrases like alabaster

urn for ashes
The whole remains

passions' black velvet
a dark still-unplanted rose

a delicate fine-penciled pastel
made gentle by abrasives

Memory reaches beyond memory
to relive it

It's a paradox to be in a body of complaints
with a mind of untouchable seasons

Vastation

At the Vastation
what you held on to may not have been worth having
—Swedenborg

Why after a fully occupied day
body sunk in drowse   mind

never finished
in a trillionth of a second

improvises a scene
an argument   a revision

as if the inner self
has slipped away

perturbed by some failure
some omission

the infinite-seeming
possibilities in infancy

a mother's joy   love's premise
unfulfilled

Why! Is there a vastation
before we die

How accept what was not
in our power to be

How be lifted by divine light
when one looks downward

the navel
the belly

the pelvis   the thighs
the knees that cannot bend

the broken feet

One Night   Two Givens

He stands aside   a guide present as witness
The line a graph of peaks and lows with finite variations

Abrupt its beginning   a birth   a note
continuing without ending   That was the first scene

then the line of a circle   all its variations
facing outward   sidewise a turning screw

seen from above a spiral
that never ascends nor descends

The third scene caused an eerie feeling
the line moved of its own volition

illimitable   gliding through airless space
until it began to curve

~

Hardly ebullience yet an affirmation
as if you can be receptive only in dreams

in suspended space   pies with hand-fluted edges
G's treble clef cut at the center

two marks on the left   three on the right
sign of balance   and that major chord: FIVE

You waked in darkness blessed
by the gradual return of predawn light

Radiance Remembered

It was yourself you blamed for mismatched
misperceived lifeworld
memory with its claws digging to unearth
  not bury flaws

We came from nowhere
came a speck   plunging   fiery
caught in a current become air
perceived   now and then
in flashes upon a beveled mirror

We are forgiven for desire
for wanting the flower   breaking its stem
carrying it upside down to hold its sap
to keep lastingly its yellow-petaled whole
Curling in upon itself   in silence it dies
accepting likely resurrection

The Light in the Eye

A man is an organ receptive of life and not life itself
  —Swedenborg

Alas
the fragrance faded from her hands

The beginning no one noticed
no witness   how could there be

Surely there was a beginning
She falls into reverie

lo   a beginning comes to her
I have known many loves

She has become her own story
born alight with possibility

a long suit
and a void

There were collisions
How could she avoid

the too hastily played card
the rock fist of others

love's piercing
dark

She asks what is sacred
answers herself

a mint stem's naked rootlets in a waterglass
a second hand clicking

folded back black wings
plunging through an ocean of air

a stab at the crown of her head
It flashed then fled into darkness

beak or beam
probing the core of what you are

not emptiness   an opening
I am not   It lives me

It lives sluicing through the body
a steady stream   a constant

Asleep the cat's ears stay perked
a drop of sound   he dashes off
                            to find what is

As if asleep enter repose
a pattern without motion

stillness in a warm room
a bluntnosed winged fish overhead
                         then beyond sound

2

Evil is *an infernal spirit that turns against itself*
—Swedenborg

She suffers putrid smells
filth the poor and insane endure

suffers seeing tracks in the snow
pawprints of a creature fleeing

Incapable of remorse a weed entwines the rose
so tight it's like rage

In gloomy depths   mouths gape
and close   gape and close

She held up a white bowl
within its watery bed of lucent pebbles
   a viper undulating toward her

Swedenborg named it
our greatest fault   selflove

She chose for herself
gorgeous turquoise-blue silk Shantung

What pleases her is beauty
and something illusive she cannot name

rushing water
his infant-like skin

Does pleasure
put the soul at risk?

How have loving kindness toward others
if she has none toward the self
   that Life itself inhabits?

Unless by *selflove*
he had sick love in mind

a disease so voracious
the more it devours the more it must consume

It feeds upon itself and the gorged host
has no choice but to serve himself

until that mortal pinprick bursts the bloat
he has become

and his soul flees

3

Resist not him who is evil
does not mean in order to suffer
                              —Tolstoy

Destroy all you possess
retreat into the frozen hinterland
   even there evil will follow you

Attack it
and it will hug you like a python

War against it
and it will become you

How abide where evil has usurped
the life of others?

In a dream you protect a furry pet
that could not protect himself

the way a mother by instinct
protects her cubs
                         tries to

If you ask a mother to accept
the unacceptable

the drugged son who nods off
the daughter who steps out
   the ninth floor window

what is it
that survives in her

When another's ways turn ugly
what can the recipient be

if not a glass bowl crashing
into the everlasting recycling bin

Oh withdraw
In solitude find the fortitude

to hold that light
that isn't light to hold

Havoc

What havoc!
even the winds and seas are in revolt
in this best of all possible worlds

where peace is only possible in intimacy
cultivate your own garden
accept what is

In quietude wait
wait till the scorpions
smug in their power

prompted by
dismal realities
self-destruct

Even goldfinches war
beak to beak in flight
despite June's bright dalliance

among needles of the Northern pine
plenteousness
shelled sunflower seed

a flutter away
from a cracked ceramic fountain
with its pretense of permanence

How brief
their overcrowding
a single female   a nibble or two

another hovers   wildly flapping
no tomorrow
no tomorrow

Safe here after their flight
eerie New York
downtown   no one

stores boarded up   graffiti

at the park ambulances waiting
white sheets

Nightmares
at sea in a small boat   an arcing
enormous wave

East Wind

Man found himself placed on a principal axis of the universe
—Pierre Teilhard de Chardin

The Present

a state without precedent and without example
—Paul Valery

Ought the black-headed grosbeak have lyrics

his body so magnificent
it's a wonder he can squeeze through
without fear of being trapped
or lookabout dread
                      the rocking cage
                      spilling seeds

the old woman listens

oppressed by angst
given what we and our father's fathers
have in ignorance
and vaingloriousness created
                      a cage
                      swaying over an abyss

as if a song could recreate mankind

Faith of Our Fathers

He who lost his father when a child professed
the Father's *undergirding power* sustained him

Citing the mystery of Joseph's fate he preached
providence shapes our ends

if we practice dependence and obedience
to His will

His daughter wonders how know His will?
Suppose the Way depends on inward sense

of the Mother's undergirding power
natural as earth is to sky

Or a third which is neither Mother nor Father
that cannot be seen   nor touched   nor heard

How can the Inscrutable resolve Turmoil
whose time has come

due to man's cross-purposes with nature
since his plow cracked rock

Family

Someone cared for you
you don't remember

Mother told you
you cried and cried and cried

when Leona became
lack

her kind of healthy
dairy farm girl

virginal and maternal
as if you were her own

explains intimate
immensity

explains why
you were never them

Reverie

Escaped
by heterodoxy

the clutch
of innocence

from birth
an insistent singularity

by instinct
told to persist

to make a bargain with what is
a constant study

pointing to the curving
forest path

that disappears
in western brilliance

Virtue

I listed all the virtues
It said *Not These*

sent the house with slatted shutters
in a scorching valley   slits of light
   reflecting in its interior pool

sent a second house   shadows
cutout shape of pomegranate
   cast upon a white wall
sound of water endlessly falling

a salubrious garden
   hanging globes of fruit
I am here   residing
the way sunlight resides in air

Death

To an old man what is more natural
than to die?
 —Cicero

Individuals die   species die
   the fleeting made eternal through incessant change
yet how unnatural it seems that eels and I
   will cease to be

Senescence—elongated   a little   age to age
   mental powers the last to decline
no excuse to be a bore   plant an English garden
   memorize French

Baudelaire   La Mort des pauvres
   C'est la clarté vibrante à notre horizon noir
C'est l'auberge fameuse inscrite sur le livre,
   Où l'on pourra manger, et dormir et s'asseoir

Recall yesterday's dream—a feast
   hosted by childhood's long gone sons
a hand embroidered cloth on which
   thrice I spilled blood red wine

Am I too blithe? too careless
   with magnet-footed crazy-paced time?
Not my expectation   a poor soul's adieu
   death as consolation

At the end of the voyage   his brain on fire
   he vows to plunge into the abyss
Au fond de L'Inconnu
   pour trouver du noueau!

The body's longing for release
   melds with its fierce grip to stay
I'll be wrenched from all I love
   but welcome death's alchemy

whether led to some high-spirited unknown
   or dissolved
perhaps reconfigured
  in another time   another place

Relic

Old and scarcity thin
a stranger came down from far north
wanting me to touch her bones
                              and know

as if what had already occurred
did not suffice

I waited below the entry
where he stood   pallid   frail

barely himself
without a voice he pleaded
Couldn't he have a bun?

This was him   my dead
                my sole love
behind him   in shadow
an age-darkened wall

where bear cub curled in upon itself
carved relic
of a people who had a myth

Love and Dust

> *if a bit of mortal, fleeting dust*
> *can make me love with faith so marvelous,*
> *how then will I love you*
>   —Petrarch's last poem

Only now do I understand
Petrarch's humble haunted prayer
So I too have loved
This day nineteen years ago

dying he looked up to me
with surprised wonder
I love you I really love you
that locked me in a too marvelous faith

Kuan Yin

Love is never finished expressing itself
It is mutilated when detached from its unrealness
                              —Gaston Bachelard

About love She was not blind
A son will go on blaming his mother
for whatever went wrong   no argument
can heal what misperception—is that the word—
                                        begot

What is love if love like hope is blind?
With an overview through time She gazes
with an inward eye
immortal being herself an image of an Image

What in the mind forgets what love
recognized would have healed
What in the human brain
auto-operates to self-harm

        You never lifted a finger
        never gave a fig how I felt

The mother too trustingly felt all was well
wherefore by omission harmed?
How detect   even by efficient intuition
what like soiled socks lay hidden
                        under a childhood bed

        Worse   worse and worse
        so deep now it can never go away

What can undo what was never done
To your own self say suffering
is what She sees   and from the dew
she collects she offers calm
                              loving calm

Mind Miniatures

April
yellow carpet sky
abundant solitude

Watchful   walking past
neglected arbors
where only flowers die

∼

Long ago and far
a girl strolling paused
captive of strange desire

a private park
crimson in tangled overgrowth
never past away

∼

After stroke returning home
three or four curb parked
electric cars

in the drive an obsidian van
on its sliding door
an inscrutable inscription

∼

Don't fret
It's just anticipatory

~

They moved me where
a fixit man in plasterwhite coveralls
sprawled on the kitchenette floor

adjacent
a new carpet   iris blue
with three prominent

squarecuts
requisitioned elsewhere
a matron

dragged remnants
mudish gray
to fit in

~

Elfinlike woman with
silverwhite hair pinkish skull
powderypale sweet faced

someone wheeling her
into a night closet
her head turns left

as if to look out
where there was no window
Do you sleep?

Sometimes
broke through
the membrane between

~

A stainless kitchen
fridge filled with bowls of sticks
groceries I thought I bought gone

a daughter brought me then went away
Hunger all day
When she returns . . . will she

Shouting   *Stock up!*
Already some are hoarding!
Already shelves are empty!

Whittled down widow
it's not contamination troubles you
it's depending for ordinary everything

~

Just get up
in this estranged body
stagger down the seafloor hall

Beyond Good and Evil

*One who perceives has great sympathy
and great contempt*
—Nietzsche

He said *Success is the greatest liar*
the ordinary gives *great advantage*

To oppose it   *the gregarious   the ignoble*
requires *immense force*

If *silenced by the judgment of others*
the creator falls into *inner desperateness*

then the drive to be healed leads to *flight*
and *forgetfulness*

Is it essential for each in her own selfhood
to be wholly dissimilar?

Isn't it the greatest difficulty to stand alone
Isn't it that he stood too high   above   beyond

self examination   a veritable
igneous floater in his eye?

*Give not that which is holy unto dogs
neither cast ye your pearls before swine*

Some are contemptible
not just commonplace   but it's the *ordinary*

he can't abide   those who *dissolve*
into the *common experience*

He had no heart for humility
a quality an inflated man cannot attain

Nietzsche   so confident
would he care?

To a Friend Who Translated the Bhagavad Gita

The eternal too late
　　　—Nietzsche

Too late the obituary came

too late to share again

the renewal that came

when we were alone together

The Library

Trunk loads in grocery bags
carrying straps that snap

What do we do with them
Dictionaries too heavy to lift

Man's Search for Meaning
in the throw-away- pile

Thousands!
Could I really have read them all

underlined   check marked   commented on
a page so frail it crumbled at my touch

Not Hopper

Not that lonely hotel room by railroad tracks
not that cafe where when the long-awaited coffee came
it lacked what the dreamer wanted

Not the Buddha-looking would-be-lover
who couldn't be embraced while the long dead one
staggered   helplessly drunk

It's all a conundrum again!

Do the dead fall into disillusionment?
Do we the living pass through
stages of belief and disbelief

then die as a spiritual teacher did
in his eyes an expression
of profound perturbation

East Wind

Even the east wind cannot bear it any longer;
it turns into a secret light...
      The Terrace of Yen
       —Li Shang-yin

Dawn already sad
I cast my net into the sea
as if coral might cling and grow

What vision
what beauty
could I leave the world

How lazy I have been!
doomed by my own nature
a cinched belt with no feeling

   ~

    a secret light

It listens
as it listened to a praying child

solely for one who is sad
for a moment

an egg-shaped pearly moonstone
emanating its own light

    there
    in your hand

then it passes

~

and enters the western sea

So earth can renew herself
and the few will be

maybe simpler
maybe wise

The harms we have done
will be like scars on rhyolite

Moss will cling to what remains

Preface

Are we atoms   merely
on a voyage from nowhere to nowhere

misguided for centuries   now
seize-the-day-ers savoring delicacies

as if the starving child's head too heavy on its bone
is as invisible as Divinity

Against Entropy

You don't talk to the dead
you talk at them
setting the story aright

a canoe overturned in rapids
belongings sodden
tied down by intention

to survive
words float to the surface
old   old   old   old   old

Oh you have come full circle
the beginning of the end
that is erasure

a pressure to speak
not chatter!   not defeated
all your mistakes stacked against you

In the no place of your somewherelse mind
you don't join the swimmers
don't join old folks for a communal meal

When the only person who calls
speaks a foreign tongue
when free association obscures your dream

a queen who could no longer be herself
being crowned
do you feel shame

thriving alongside humanity's crimes
against life   the shame
of a good enough fortune?

Life   *human* life   For Hawking
an equivalent *in all the universe*
unlikely   Feel it! that pressure

to evolve
to become a paradigm
of compassion

to grow in spiritual insight
to find eternal life
alight within

Fog

Nothing could be discerned
in its porous density

Stooping over I tried to imprint
something important

A black glove gripped my wrist
I screamed

Don't scream　he said　almost
as if to reassure me

Awake
I could not go back to sleep

could not call up his image
The driver?　sent

just as I had begun
to imagine more

Meditation on The Big Bang

Suppose at that instant afterward
the strong nuclear and the weak
                      —prone to entropy—
combined with electromagnetic force
   as physicists propose

the gravitational fourth so slight it hardly mattered
though it holds us like a god in its hands

while the immanent bellows blows galaxies
   spiraling languorously
farther and farther and farther apart

the long exhale of a Titan's breath
until that cavernous lung empties
                            halts

a split in time
              Wham!

and the Immanent Will begins a long deep inhale

Aubade II

Upward from the damp
spore-aired forest floor

an ibis-white light burst
between the thighs of tree

on its blue dot
in the cosmic rainbow

Little Season

*an angel came down
the key of the bottomless pit
and a great chain in his hand*

*after a thousand years
he must be loosed*
                —Revelations

*Often in the obscure being,
dwells a hidden God*
                —Nerval

What Dwells Within

A handmade ceramic fountain planted with desert flora
each in its tiny eloquent identity   succulent greens
blush oranges   hints of orpiment yellow
at its height a multi-fingered upthrust
glorying in no more   no lesser life

comforted me
after a night by dismal thought besieged
and morning pain a boulder
blocking the rushing deathward flow

>   *just be*

what dwells within
whispered me
pool here   in my depths

By Birth Conferred

When blasted by reverberations
from another's annealed hurt
no nurturance ever could nor can cure
love twists upon itself and burns

Am I weak   am I water   a Pisces' pair
heading disparate directions
How heal a soul with a keen knife
that merely cuts water

How heal when what ought to be
by birth conferred
curls in upon itself   scorched
blackened like paper in fire

Extricate Yourself

Her irrational fits
(face distorted aged and grim)

strike through me
I tremble   can't breathe

You must extricate yourself
wakes me in a dream

In a dream I saw
seven wheeling golden disks

but I did not know
how to extricate myself

In a poem I read
to save yourself

you must go beyond
self and suffering

Something . . . my state—
an inexplicable change

when we met again
I heard the surreal voice

I have stamped the seal of approval
onto your forehead

Her face softened   being herself Joy
and I saw Beauty

Psilocybin

At night mind's manacled to failures
brain's old mini grooves

In dream's little melodrama
I step down up to my neck in a flat field of snow

evidence of imperfect perception
and ego's

god-usurping volition

Must I kneel to a mushroom
to attain grace

ecstasy in warm embrace
all-inclusive love

dissolving bliss
to be not being one's self

being no being at all

I sip my twice-warmed coffee
pain in remission

The rain-enlivened plant
flares its purple petals

drinking in noonlight
not I

an ephemeral liberation

Spirit

Spirit   resides
ever evolving
finding itself
expressing itself

in a house in a valley shimmering
in one-hundred-degree heat
through its slatted shutters
reflecting upon a sheltered pool

in another   no images
but cutout shapes   pomegranates
cast upon a white wall
the sound of water endlessly falling

in Eve's garden
in an ancient olive grove
in imagination
it abides

My Slipper

The way I've been seeking isn't hallucinatory
Not to lose the past or dwell in it
Not expecting splendor before I die

Not possessions   special as the beige slipper
found after a year's intermittent search
replica of the old ones that fell apart

In the midst of cooking beef bourguignon
I glance down—a spot   oil!
rush to the shoebox of polishes and buffers

grab a black-capped can and spray
a finger-length away
a blotch of saturated black

Now I wear my slipper with its mark
grateful for its interior furry warmth
in this time of winter rain and cold

Clumsy

rises out of the blue to judge you
the way words   being neutral   do

Knocked by airy nothing
a Martha Stewart carton
flips from your grip

coq au vin   a galactic splatter

a betrayal of continuity
this mocking gesture
comes just to say

don't imagine you are what you have been

Penitent

My soul is sore vexed
—Psalm 6

How hideous it was!
the way my good friend abraded me

accused me   that I the host
kept the bread secretly for myself

And his wife   also my friend
stood by   watching in silence

Of course it was not him but animus
my own turned against me

How long have I suffered anger
caused by incapacity of self-defense

Even now I value harmony
and cannot   even when I try

in daylight
speak double-ax words

Gnosis

When you get seriously old dreams vacate nowhere
If you're lucky just as daybreak pink seeps between a needles' eye
a yellow jack knife   suspended there

       simulacrum of Jerry's red army knife
       the airport servant flung into his authorized bin

nights later   *two peppers*
one orange   one yellow

       yellow dragon   a favorable sign
       yellow as the golden mean
       alchemy's transit _ : ' ' '

       orange as the monks' unison
       signifying fire

Steadily your hand holds the broadest knife
slicing veggies   giving each its own shape
concentrating to cut and separate

Candor

*I am too alone in the world, and yet not alone enough
to make every moment holy.*
—Book of Hours, Rilke

The alabaster urn that once held ashes
resides alongside books no longer
able to pacify my mind
and the animal no longer frisky
paces herself to fit the end

When the world feels unholy
I invoke white   a tint called *permanent*
to accommodate the surface
wavering with tension
ringing at the bronze bowl's rim

What greater music comes

At the Verge

There is a verge of the mind which these things haunt.
—William James

The meaningful coincidence or equivalence of a psychic and a physical state that have no causal relationship...is a modality without a cause, an 'acausal orderedness'.
—C. G. Jung

had she not cut my throat
had I not caught a cold
had I not been hours away
had there been no other delay

Together   mother and son
walked the path above Carmel's shore
in the calm of a sea that has no shore
That night my chronic cough caused by an impatient
scalpel severing the sphincter muscle
became nightlong cough-linked-to-cough

Given the warning I was at high risk
of pneumonia   at dawn   suppressing dread
I drove north past sequestered towns
the land itself gone still

At nine the triage room looked empty
An aid laid me down on a bed
as predicted my lungs were infected
Expecting to be released on the cell to my daughter
the car's parked on the fifth floor!
on the fifth floor!
the curtain   opened   closed   opened
opened to crazed comings and goings

frusstrated   my wingedarm waving   *clozzz clozz*
flinging myself forward   slurring   *privvvvacyyyy*

male voice
you are having a stroke

2

A happy Santa wheels me into his angelic white van
with his handsome dark-eyed ingéneu
we laugh and joke
his siren singing he whisks us over the bridge
an elevator up to the fifth floor
a monstrous machine huge as the room
under its brow a nurse bends over
punctures my groin   torments a vein
snaking up   up into my brain
silence
more silence
nothing moves

bass voice   *I am going*
to abort   the massive bloodclot
has dissolved

3

My veins cut   taped bleeding
antibiotic acid burning up my age-thinned skin

exhausted I fell down and down into the pit
of deep sleep

waked-up   waked-up   waked-up
what rest?

my writs's bled into the flimsy gown
blood-damp   cold

legs and arms wrapped in icemelt
cold   why so cold

so alone

down on your knees
winter's cold floor   a prayer

spoken aloud in the gown of night
to no.one

This must be what dying is
lie still   wait

for no.one

*And fire came down
out of the heavens*

I was held down
pythons tightened around my limbs

then   for no reason
released into darkness

gloved fingers forced
wide open my eyelids

light pierced my right eye
light pierced my left eye
Your name! your name!
Your birthdate

Where are you
Why are you here

The devils came every two hours
nights and days and nights

Daylight

A bright-faced black man offers a selection

rubberized croissant microwaved omelet
tries again   three soft-boiled eggs

hunger
I must be well

My daughter full of light
It was only forty-eight hours

then the explanation   the lucky timing
her required permission

a blood-thinner cocktail that
could have caused my demise

Blessed to be alive
not blind   not paralyzed

yet I worried
she was taking me where

another book was opened
which is the book of life

No.one intervened in my fate
What—then—is expected of me?

The Expectation

No   I was wrong   There is a beginning and there is an end
Eternal time is now and never

Ask your (dead) parents
Your carry-all is gone

Your black cat has a fatal condition
Your best friend isn't any more

What is expected of when day is fogwhite
Absolute quiet on this side of glass

Late spring cold   ground no pickax can penetrate
Each mistake left its scar

Nothing is expected of you
Nothing is

No   That is wrong   Now is
all that is

The oriole and the mourning doves
have returned

About the Author

Phyllis Stowell is Professor Emerita from Saint Mary's College and Founding Member of the SMC MFA, and recently retired Chair, Friends of the C. G. Jung Institute of San Francisco. Her poetry appeared in over 40 reviews, both traditional and experimental. After her BA, she earned an MA in creative writing at SF State, where she studied with Robert Creeley, Stan Rice, and the Greek poet/writer Nanos Valaoritis. Later she earned a Ph.D. in Poetry and Depth Psychology. The marvelous poet Robert Hass was a participant in her Ph.D. Committee. Her residencies include Hedgebrook Farm, Djerassi, MacDowell Colony, Camargo Foundation (Cassis, France), Virginia Center for the Creative Arts, and CAMAC, Centre d'Art (Marnay-sur-seine, France). She is a widow and lives in Berkeley, California, with Ravi, her black Persian cat.